# Everything You Need To Know About
# GROWING UP
# MALE

Sharing experiences with your male friends can help you learn a lot about yourself.

# Everything You Need To Know About
# GROWING UP MALE

## Bruce S. Glassman

*Series Editor:* Evan Stark, Ph.D.

THE ROSEN PUBLISHING GROUP, INC.
NEW YORK

Published in 1991 by The Rosen Publishing Group, Inc.
29 East 21st Street, New York, New York 10010

First Edition
Copyright © 1991 by The Rosen Publishing Group, Inc.

Manufactured in the United States of America.

Library of Congress Cataloging-in-Publication Data

Glassman, Bruce.
    Everything you need to know about growing up male/Bruce S. Glassman.—1st ed.
    (The Need to know library)
    Includes bibliographical references and index.
    Summary: Examines the physical and psychological changes that teenage boys experience as they grow into manhood and discusses such aspects as grooming, social responsibilities and pressures, and sexual behavior.
    ISBN 0-8239-1224-8
    1. Sex instruction for boys.  2. Puberty—Juvenile literature.
3. Hygiene, Sexual—Juvenile literature.  [1. Sex instruction for boys.
2. Puberty.  3. Teenage boys.]  I. Title.  II. Series.
HO41.G53   1991
613.9'53—dc20                                              90-25878
                                                                CIP
                                                                 AC

# Contents

# Introduction

Who are you? You are actually many different things. You are the child of two individual people. Maybe you are a brother to some other people. You are a certain age. You go to school in a specific place. These are all things that help to make you the person you are. There are other things, too.

If you are a male, you have special body characteristics. You share those traits only with other males. You are treated in a certain way because you are male. You have special fears and problems in growing up male. Your life as a male is what this book is about.

Throughout history people have been shaped a good deal by their sex (gender). As time has passed, men and women have been treated more and more alike. A hundred years ago there were no female politicians. Fifty years ago, no male would ever be a receptionist in an office.

Today, jobs cannot be only for men or only for women. Any job is open to both sexes. The people we look up to today include female doctors, male clothing designers, female police officers, and male "househusbands." But there are many other roles that we play. Think about the way you are expected to behave with other people. Think about how you are expected to behave with other boys. Think about how you are expected to behave with girls. Do you think you are expected to behave differently with girls than with boys?

There are many things about men and women that are different. But there are more things that are alike. The purpose of this book is not to prove that men and women are totally different. And it is certainly not to prove that being a man is any better or worse than being a woman. The purpose of this book is to show that growing up male is a very special experience. And, as a man, it is important to understand that experience in order to understand yourself.

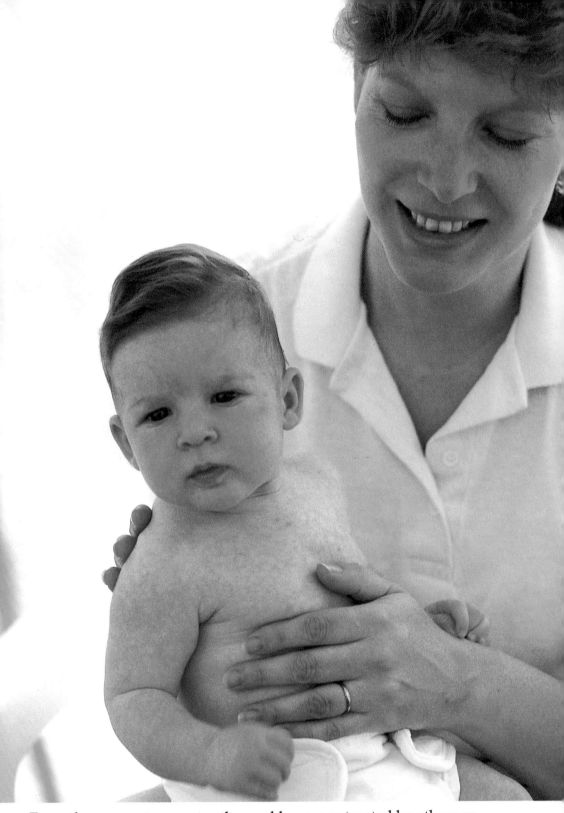

From the moment you enter the world, you are treated by others as a male.

# Chapter 1

# What It Means to Be Male

From the time they are born, boys and girls are treated differently. Girls can wear dresses. Boys don't. Boys' bikes have a bar across the top. Girls' bikes don't. Boys have one locker room. Girls have a different one.

Boy babies and girl babies are different at birth. Every boy has a penis. Every girl has a vagina. But there is a time when male and female bodies change a great deal. That time is called puberty. After puberty, boys and girls look very different from one another.

## What Is Puberty?

Puberty is a time of great change. For most boys it starts at about age twelve. It usually lasts until about age seventeen. But puberty can start as early as age ten or as late as age fifteen. Every boy's body is different. Each body will develop at its own speed. Whatever the speed, your body will begin to grow in surprising ways. At puberty, your body's chemicals tell your body how to grow.

Puberty means many of the same things for boys and girls. For both it means growing taller. For both it means body hair will grow. And it means that muscles will develop and become stronger. Both boys and girls will probably get pimples and oily hair. And both will begin to have body odors (smells) they never had before.

Body changes are not the only changes during puberty. Many changes are emotional. You will have new feelings about yourself and about sex. These feelings are very confusing. Many people become very upset by the rush of feelings they have during puberty. All of a sudden you are growing taller. You are getting pimples on your face. Your voice is cracking. You are becoming a different person. These changes can be scary if you do not know what to expect.

Once puberty begins, most young people start to think about sex. Many of the changes in your body at puberty are to get the body ready to have sex. They make a boy able to have *intercourse* (sex). They make you able to *reproduce* (get a female pregnant).

## Going through Puberty

Changes in your body during puberty come in stages. The stages are usually the same for every boy. But the order of the stages is not always the same. And each boy will go through puberty in his own special way.

For some boys, the first sign they see is hair around the penis and the scrotum (sac under the penis). This is called *pubic hair.* Other boys notice that their penises grow larger first. Still other boys begin to grow taller before they see pubic hair.

Whatever the order, your puberty will take its own course. You should not worry if you are not growing in the same ways as your friends. Or as fast. Your body has its own schedule.

Sometimes it is hard to compare yourself to other boys. In the locker room, you may feel embarrassed if you don't have any pubic hair and the other boys do. You may feel embarrassed if you *do* have pubic hair and the other boys *don't.* Whatever the case, just remember that thinking of body parts as "better" or "worse" is silly. Everyone's body is different. That's what makes us each unique. Besides, you don't control the way you grow. The chemicals in your body control that. You have inherited your body from your parents. And the way those chemicals work comes from your parents, too.

## The Stages of Puberty

There is no set time for puberty. Every person is different. But there are general rules. Most boys will start to see the first signs at about age twelve. If you begin to see signs at age ten, don't worry. If you don't see anything by age thirteen, don't worry. It probably just means that your body takes an early or late start to do its job.

There are five stages of puberty.

**Stage One:**   This starts at birth. It continues through childhood. During this time your penis, scrotum (testicle sac), and testicles do not change very much. You do not have much hair on your body. Your muscles and bones are still in their earliest stage.

**Stage Two:**   This usually starts around ages eleven to thirteen. Then changes become easier to see. During this time your testicles will start to get bigger. Your scrotum will begin to hang lower. Your penis will begin to get bigger, too. But the penis will not grow as much as the testicles and the scrotum.

Stage two usually takes about thirteen months. But it is normal for it to take anywhere from five months to about two years.

**Stage Three:**   At this stage your penis will get bigger. It will get longer and wider. Your scrotum and testicles will continue to grow. You may notice that one of your testes ("balls") hangs lower than the other. This is normal. It happens so they don't crush each other when you walk. You may also notice that one testicle is larger than the other. This is normal too. It is because one testicle is growing faster than the other. When you are an adult they should be about the same size.

You may also notice the beginning of pubic hair. Small, dark, curly hairs will grow around your penis and your scrotum. As puberty continues, pubic hair will get thicker. By the time you are an adult it will cover your *crotch* (the area between your legs, where your penis and scrotum are).

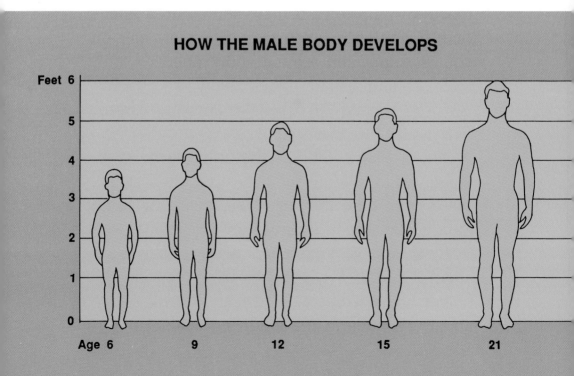

**HOW THE MALE BODY DEVELOPS**

Feet 6
5
4
3
2
1
0

Age 6    9    12    15    21

Stage Three usually takes about ten months. But it is normal for it to take anywhere from two to nineteen months.

**Stage Four:**  By this stage your penis has grown quite a lot.  It is the last stage where major growth occurs.  The skin on your penis and your scrotum will also be getting deeper in color.  Oil and sweat glands will develop. *Glands* are organs that release different liquids in the body.  The oils that you see on your face when you are a teen are released by glands. The sweat under your arms also comes from glands.  There are oil and sweat glands on your penis as well.

By now you will probably have a good deal of pubic hair.  Many young men have pubic hair that grows up toward their belly button and onto their thighs.  You may also grow hair on your scrotum and around your anus.

Stage four usually takes about two years. But it is normal for it to take anywhere from five months to three years.

**Stage Five:**  This is the fully-grown adult stage.  Many young men have reached stage five by the time they are sixteen. Other young men do not reach it until they are about twenty.

By this stage your penis will probably be about 3 1/4 to 4 1/4 inches long.  It will be longer when it becomes erect.  We will talk about erections in the following chapters.

## What Happens to Girls during Puberty

This book is about boys. But it is important to have some information about girls, too. Many boys are curious about the changes in a girl's body during puberty. And it is comforting to know that you are not the only one whose body is changing. You may be less embarrassed around girls if you know that they are going through great changes too.

Puberty happens in stages for girls, too. And female puberty is a lot like male puberty. Both sexes grow a great deal. Girls and boys both grow pubic hair. And they both have sweat glands and oil glands that start to work.

For boys, puberty means the growth of sex organs. That is true for girls as well. One of the first changes for girls during puberty is the growth of the breasts. It is during this time that the breasts grow bigger and change shape. The nipples become darker in color. And the area around the nipples stands out more.

During puberty, boys first produce sperm. For girls, puberty means producing the first "ripe" eggs from their *ovaries*. When a woman is born, she already has all her eggs in her ovaries. As the female gets older, her eggs become more mature. During puberty, the eggs get ready to be released. Each month one egg is released.

Two things can happen when the egg is released. The egg can become fertilized by sperm, if the woman has had sex. The woman would then be pregnant. We will talk more about how this happens in the next chapter.

If the egg is not fertilized, it will dissolve. The dissolved egg will then be flushed out of the body. Blood will carry the egg out through the vagina. This bleeding from the vagina is called *menstruation* (having a "period"). A woman may be slightly uncomfortable during her period. This is not because of the bleeding. It is because a woman's body stores more water before her period. This can cause headaches, cramps, and swelling (bloating). A woman who is not pregnant gets her period about every 28 days (once a month).

During her period, a woman may use something to stop the blood from flowing out of the vagina. This is called a *tampon*. It is made out of absorbent fiber and paper. It is inserted into the vagina, where it soaks up the blood. A tampon has a little string at the end of it. This sticks out of the vagina. The tampon is removed by pulling on the string. Some women use *sanitary napkins* ("maxi-pads") instead of tampons. These are not inserted into the vagina. They are placed over the outside of the vagina. There they absorb the blood as it comes out of the vagina.

## Feelings about Beginning Puberty

You will probably have mixed feelings about starting puberty. Like your friends, you will be excited and scared at the same time.

Part of you will probably be happy to think about growing up. The start of puberty means that you will soon be a man. You will have more responsibility, more independence, more freedom. It means that you will be treated more like an adult.

Part of you may be excited about looking different. Growing your first moustache can be fun. Getting taller and having your muscles grow stronger, can also be exciting.

But all these changes can be scary, too. You will probably feel that you are not ready for all the changes at once. You may not want your penis to grow big and hairy. And who wants his face to have pimples? Or your underarms to be sweaty? But these things are normal. And mixed feelings about puberty are normal. Just remember that puberty is a natural part of growing up. It is as natural as breathing and eating. Try thinking of your body as a wonderful machine. Respect the things your body can do. You will be amazed at how your body knows just when to start puberty and what to do during puberty.

Boys come in many shapes and sizes. During puberty, every boy grows at his own rate.

# Chapter 2

---

# What Makes Puberty Work?

We know from chapter 1 that many changes happen to your body during puberty. Many of those changes you can see. But the chemicals that cause those changes are deep inside your body.

## Hormones

Puberty does different things to boys and girls. That's because boys and girls have different chemicals inside their bodies. These chemicals are called *hormones*. Hormones cause the body to change during puberty. The most important male hormone for puberty is called *testosterone*. This hormone makes your penis grow. It makes hair grow on your chest, legs, and face. It makes muscles grow strong and heavy. It causes the *testicles* ("balls") to produce *sperm*. Once a boy begins making sperm he is *fertile*. His sperm can make a girl pregnant.

## Being Able to Have Sex

Many of the changes your body makes during puberty are to get you ready for sex. Men and women *reproduce* by having sex. To reproduce means to have a baby. But having babies is not the only reason that people have sex. Many people have sex because it is a special part of loving someone else.

Sex is a very hard issue to talk about. That is because many people have many different beliefs about it. Some people say sex should only be for making babies. Other people say it can be just for pleasure. Still other people say you should only have sex when you are married. Other people say you can have sex with someone you care about. You will have many decisions to make when you are old enough to have sex. You will have to decide what is right for you. Before we talk more about sex, we must talk about how the male body works.

## The Male Body

The most important sex organs you have are the penis and the testicles. The penis is made up of the *shaft* and the *glans.* The glans is the top part of the penis. The glans is also called the "head" of the penis. There is a slit at the very tip of the penis. This is the *urinary opening.* When you urinate ("piss"), the liquid comes out of this opening. The urinary opening also passes a liquid during sex.

A penis can be any one of many shapes and sizes. Some penises are short and thick. Others are long and thin. Some penises are *circumcised*. That means that skin over the top part of the penis has been trimmed. The skin is called *foreskin*. Boys are usually circumcised when they are two or three days old.

Today most boys are circumcised. It is done regularly in hospitals. For many people, circumcision is a religious ceremony. Jews and Muslims circumcise their boys for religious reasons. But you do not have to be Jewish or Muslim to be circumcised. Many people believe there are health benefits to being circumcised. But the health benefits have not been definitely proved.

If you are not circumcised, it is important to keep the area under your foreskin clean. You should pull back the foreskin when you bathe or shower. Then wash under it. If you don't clean under your foreskin, there will be a build-up of *smegma*. Smegma is released by glands in the penis. If smegma is not washed out regularly, it can build up. When smegma builds up, it can cause an unpleasant odor. Or it can cause a rash.

The *testicles* (or testes) are held inside a sac called the *scrotum*. The testicles are often

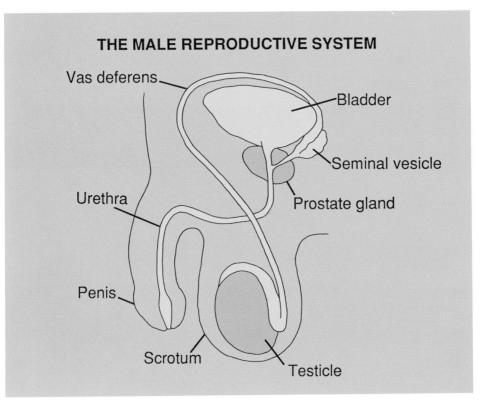

**THE MALE REPRODUCTIVE SYSTEM**

Vas deferens

Bladder

Seminal vesicle

Urethra

Prostate gland

Penis

Scrotum

Testicle

called "balls," or "nuts." This is because they are two small, round objects. The testes produce sperm. Sperm is the male "seed" for making babies. Your body begins to make sperm during the first stages of puberty.

The testes are made up of hundreds of yards of tiny coiled tubing. The sperm is made inside this tubing. Sperm are alive. And they are very tiny. You cannot see them with the naked eye. When they are fully mature, they look like tadpoles (newborn frogs). A sperm has a big head and a long wiggly tail. Each sperm carries *genes* inside its head. Genes are the chemicals that tell your body how to grow, and what to make you look like. You were created by genes from your mother and father. That is why you have many things that your parents have. Like the color of your hair. Or your nose. Or your height. The genes inside *your* sperm will carry physical traits too.

On top of the testes is a compartment called the *epididymis*. Sperm made in the testicles mature in the compartment. When they are mature ("ripe"), they travel upwards. The ripe sperm travel through a long tube called the *vas deferens*. The ripe sperm travel to the *ampulla*. The ampulla holds the sperm until they are ready to be *ejaculated*. When you ejaculate, your penis releases a milky white fluid, called *semen*. Semen is a mixture of sperm and other fluids produced by the *seminal vesicles*. Only a tenth of that liquid is actually sperm. On average, about a teaspoon of semen is ejaculated.

Ejaculation is also called *orgasm*. That is because ejaculation is caused by a series of muscle spasms in the penis. As the muscles contract and relax, they push the semen out of the penis. Some people use the word "come" when they mean "orgasm." Sometimes people also use this word for the fluid that is released by ejaculation. These are slang terms.

## Erections

Your penis has to be erect before you can ejaculate. When your penis gets hard and stiff, that is called an *erection*. Slang words for an erection are "hard on," and "boner." You can get an erection for many different reasons. It happens most often because you are sexually excited. Thoughts about sex can give you an erection. Being touched can give you an erection. Having your pants rub against your penis can give you an erection. You can get an erection without even thinking about it.

When you have an erection, it feels like your penis is a bone. But there is no bone. Your penis is made up of soft, spongy tissue. Your penis gets erect when the spongy tissue fills up with blood. As it fills up, pressure is created inside the penis. The pressure and the blood make the penis stand up. When you are ready to ejaculate, the pressure inside your penis will make it possible. The muscles will contract, and put pressure on the tube that carries the sperm (the vas deferens). As the vas deferens is squeezed, the semen will come out through the urinary opening at the tip of your penis.

## Wet Dreams

Sperm has already been made by your body before your first ejaculation. Sperm is constantly made by your body every day. It is stored in your ampulla. When the ampulla becomes full, it needs to empty itself. It needs to make room for new sperm.

Often the ampulla will empty itself while you are sleeping. It will cause you to have an erection. Then it will cause you to ejaculate. This is commonly known as a "wet dream."

Wet dreams can be scary if you don't expect them. That is because you wake up and find a wet spot on your underwear or your bedsheets. You may feel embarrassed, because it feels like you "wet your bed." Or you may feel embarrassed because you were dreaming of something sexy. But wet dreams are perfectly normal. Every boy will have at least one during puberty. For many boys it will be their first ejaculation. Wet dreams show you that you are a healthy, growing male.

## Masturbation

*Masturbation* means exciting yourself. If you are a male, most of the time masturbation means exciting your penis. Often masturbation is done to reach orgasm. There are many ways to masturbate. Some people touch themselves in ways that feel good. Other people excite themselves while they daydream about sex.

Some people are against masturbation for religious reasons. Many people are against masturbation because they feel it is shameful.

Other people, however, say masturbation is a normal and healthy thing. Some people use masturbation to become better lovers. They use it to explore their own bodies. Masturbation is usually done alone.

The decision to masturbate is a choice. If you choose to masturbate, you should not feel guilty. Both men and women masturbate. Married people and single people masturbate. And people who have regular, active sex lives with partners also masturbate.

## The Female Body

From the outside, you can see the lips of a woman's vagina. There are outer lips and inner lips. The *clitoris* is a small organ near the outside of the vagina hidden by folds of skin. The clitoris is very sensitive. The folds of skin inside the vagina protect the clitoris. During sex, the penis pushes back the folds. The pressure of the penis on the clitoris gives pleasure to the woman.

From the outside you can also see the opening of the *vagina*. The vagina is like a collapsed tube. The vagina is a passageway to the *uterus*. The uterus (or "womb") is where babies grow before they are born. Two tubes run down into the uterus. One comes from the left, one from the right. These are the *fallopian tubes*. They carry the eggs from the ovaries.

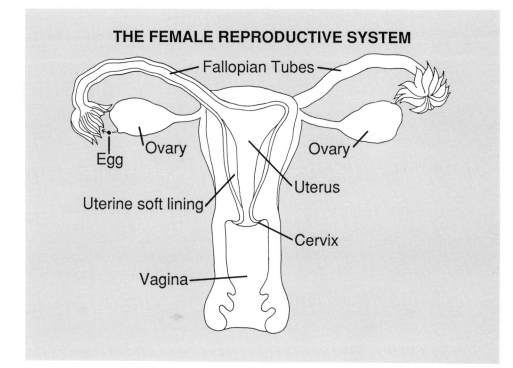

THE FEMALE REPRODUCTIVE SYSTEM

Fallopian Tubes

Ovary

Egg

Ovary

Uterus

Uterine soft lining

Cervix

Vagina

Each woman has two ovaries. One is connected to the left fallopian tube. The other is connected to the right.

Each month, one of the ovaries releases an egg. These eggs are very, very small. You cannot see them with the naked eye. You need a microscope. The egg travels down the fallopian tube and lands in the uterus. If the egg has been fertilized by sperm, it will connect itself to the wall of the uterus. This is the beginning of pregnancy. If the egg has not been fertilized, it will dissolve. Then it will be flushed out in the flow of blood called menstruation ("the period").

## How Pregnancy Happens

Pregnancy can happen when a man and a woman have sex (intercourse). Men and women can have sex without getting pregnant. One way is to use birth control. We will talk about birth control in Chapter 4.

A man must have an erection in order to have sex with a woman. Often both the man and the woman get excited by *foreplay*. The object of foreplay is to get both partners excited and ready for intercourse. It is a time to kiss and touch each other. When the man is excited, he will get an erection. When the woman is excited, her vagina will become moist (wet) by releasing fluids. This usually means she is ready for intercourse. These fluids make it easier to insert the penis into the vagina.

When the man has an erection, he is ready to insert his penis into the woman's vagina. The penis is very sensitive. It becomes more excited inside the vagina. If it is excited enough, it will ejaculate. The man will have an orgasm. The semen will shoot out of the penis and into the vagina.

The sperm begin swimming from the vagina up to the uterus. From the uterus they travel to the fallopian tubes. Some sperm swim up the left tube. Some swim up the right tube. The sperm are now heading for the ovaries.

As we know, an egg is released each month from the ovaries. When it is released, the egg travels down the fallopian tube. It is possible for the sperm to meet the egg along the way. If this happens, *fertilization* is almost certain. There is an easy way to understand fertilization. Think of the sperm as carrying half a seed. The egg carries the other half. When the sperm and the egg join, there is a whole seed. A whole seed can begin to grow. When a whole seed can grow, we say it is fertilized. And we say the woman who carries that seed is pregnant. It only takes one sperm to fertilize the egg. Millions and millions of sperm are released in each ejaculation.

Sperm can live for three to four days inside a woman's body. When an egg is released from the ovary, it usually can be fertilized for about three days. If a man and a woman have unprotected sex around the time that the egg is released, chances for pregnancy are very high. Any time a man and a woman have unprotected sex, chances for pregnancy are high. Chances become higher closer to the time the egg is released from the ovaries.

If an egg is fertilized, it travels to the uterus. The fertilized egg attaches to the wall of the uterus. There it begins to grow. In nine months it will be a baby, ready to be born.

## Thoughts about Sex

Erections and wet dreams are part of growing up. Most of the time you cannot control them. That is because your hormones are controlling them for you. Your hormones will also make you start thinking about sex more often. Now that your body is ready to have sex, it will signal your brain to think about sex.

Thinking about sex can be very scary. Sex means being very close to someone. And doing things that are very personal. Thinking about your first time is also very scary. You will have to make many decisions about sex. And you will have to think about the dangers of AIDS and STDs. Some people want to wait to have sex until they are married. Others want to be in love. Others are curious, and want to enjoy sex as soon as possible. Your parents have their opinion. So does your rabbi or your pastor. Your teachers may offer advice. And your friends will certainly have an opinion. Talk about sex with people you trust. You can learn a lot from them.

### How do you make sense of it all?

It is important to remember this: Sex is a very personal matter. You should not have sex, if you don't want to, under pressure from your friends. You need to consider and respect the opinions of your parents and teachers. But in the end you must decide what is right for you.

# Chapter 3

## Taking Care of Yourself

Y ou cannot stop the changes of puberty. But you can take good care of yourself. A good diet helps. So does plenty of exercise and good *hygiene* (keeping your body clean). Remember, puberty is natural. And everyone goes through it. The more you know about it, the easier it will be.

Let's talk about each of the major changes of puberty. And let's find out how we can make them easier to live with.

### Zits, Blackheads, and Other Skin Problems

There are many things you can do to keep pimples (zits) under control.

Pimples begin to appear more often during puberty, when your skin gets oilier. Most pimples are caused by *sebum*. Sebum is produced by your oil glands. You have oil glands all over your body. You have many oil glands on your face, neck, shoulders, chest, and back. Your skin is made up of millions of tiny openings. These openings are called *pores*. If you look at your face up close in the mirror, you can see them. Sebum travels from your glands to your pores. During puberty, your glands are making a lot of sebum. Often the sebum clogs your pores. When this happens, a pimple forms.

When a pore is clogged, you will get a pimple. Sometimes it is a *blackhead*. Many people think blackheads are little pieces of dirt in the pore. That is not true. Blackheads are sebum stuck in your pores. When the sebum is exposed to air, it sometimes turns black.

Other pimples are called *whiteheads*. Whiteheads are sebum too. They are sebum trapped right under the surface of the skin.

Eight out of every ten teens have mild skin problems during puberty. Some people have a more serious problem called *acne*. Acne pimples get infected and swollen. They may also cause scars to form. Acne tends to come from your family. If your parents had acne, you might have it too.

Your diet influences how you look. Greasy, fatty "junk" foods can contribute to oily skin and cause pimples.

Many teens get upset by their pimples. They feel like the zits will never go away. Many teens think they have acne. But acne is a very severe case of pimples and infections. Most teens do not have real acne. If you are worried about acne, you should see a doctor. A doctor that treats skin problems is called a *dermatologist.* A dermatologist can give you medication that will help with acne.

## How Can You Ease Pimple Problems?

There are a number of things you can do to keep your pimples under control. But pimples will still appear. You should try not to be upset. Eventually your pimples will go away.

### The foods you eat

Many doctors believe that some foods can make pimples worse. Some doctors disagree with this idea. But a good diet will help you feel well. When you feel well, you can deal with the pressures of school and your personal life. Pay attention to how your body reacts. Some foods may cause you to "break out" more than others. If you pay attention to what you eat, you will know what foods to cut out.

Many doctors say that greasy foods can cause more pimples. These foods include french fries, potato chips, and other deep fried foods. Some people think chocolate can cause pimples. Others think salty foods make pimples worse. None of these foods are very good for anybody's diet. And none of them should make up a large part of what you eat each day. You should stop eating foods like these if you see that they make you break out.

Your diet is important in many ways. Remember, your body is doing a lot of work during puberty. This work requires good fuel. Vitamin-rich foods and low-fat foods are the best fuel for the body.

## Stress

A good diet will also help you deal with *stress.* Stress is the pressure you feel from all the things you worry about. Stress can cause pimples too. You get stress from school, from worrying about sex, from problems with your parents. Sometimes stress builds up. Then the body is strained. You may feel tired and break out more than usual. Exercise is a good way to release stress. That is because stress is often stored in tense muscles. Exercise helps to tire and relax those muscles.

## Keeping your face clean

Many people think that pimples come from having a dirty face. That is not true. You can wash your face every day and still get pimples.

Hygiene means taking care of yourself. Washing your face and hair every day helps control pimples and oily hair.

But daily washing can help control pimples. Washing removes extra oils from the skin. This helps to keep the pores open. It is best to wash with warm water. Warm water opens your pores. Rinse with cold water when you are done. Cold water closes your pores.

One important note: Don't pop pimples with your fingers or other tools. Squeezing and poking your face can cause scars. Infections and irritations can develop. It is best to keep your face clean and let pimples run their course. It is hard to be patient when you have pimples. But they will go away faster if you leave them alone.

## Body Odors

Once puberty starts, your sweat glands work harder. You sweat all over your body. But some places are more easily seen than others. Under your arms, in your crotch, and your feet are places you sweat a lot. The sweat from these areas often smells bad.

We all sweat when we are nervous. Often that sweat smells very strong. What you eat makes a difference, too. If you eat garlic, your sweat will smell like garlic. Many teens spend a lot of time being nervous. And this means teens sweat a lot.

A good way to control body odor is to take a shower or a bath daily. You can also use a deodorant or an anti-perspirant after you wash. You usually spray or rub a deodorant under your arms. This covers up your natural odor with an artificial odor. Anti-perspirants are different. They contain a chemical that soaks up your sweat. Some people are afraid that the chemical then soaks into your skin. This has not been proven. But many people feel anti-perspirants are not healthy.

Wearing clean clothes will also help control body odor. It is best to wear a shirt only once before it is washed. The same is true for socks and underwear. Fresh clothes will help you smell fresh and clean.

## Taking Care of Your Hair

We have already mentioned that your hair will be oilier during puberty. But everyone's hair is different. Maybe your hair will seem greasy after one day. Maybe it will not seem greasy after two days. It's a good idea to wash your hair every day if your hair is very oily. But if you wash your hair too much, this can dry it out. When your hair is dry it breaks easily.

Some people develop *dandruff*. Dandruff is little white flakes that fall out of your hair. These are small flakes of dead skin from your scalp. Sometimes dandruff itches. Having dandruff does not mean that your hair is dirty. It just means you need to use a shampoo that controls dandruff. There are many dandruff shampoos in the drugstore. Ask your druggist which one is best for you.

## Shaving

For many young men, their first shave is an exciting event. Shaving can make you feel grown up. It's something your dad does. And now you can do it too.

The first hairs you see on your face will probably be over your upper lip. Then you may see hair growing along your ears (sideburns). Eventually, hair will start to grow all over your cheeks and chin.

Your first shave can be an exciting event in your life. It is proof that you are growing up.

When you start to shave is up to you. It depends on how much hair you have on your face. Some young men choose not to shave the hair as it grows over their lips. They like to leave it. It is a sign that they are growing up. Other young men can't wait to buy a razor of their own.

It is best to shave after you shower. That way your face is warm and wet. And your pores are more open.

There are two ways to shave. One way is to use a regular razor with a blade. To do that you also need shaving cream. Shaving this way takes practice. You must be careful not to cut yourself. It is best to have someone show you how to shave this way.

The other way to shave is easier. You can use an electric razor. You do not need shaving cream. There are some lotions you can use before you shave. They are used to reduce the irritation of shaving.

Shaving can irritate (scrape) your skin. Often it can cause pimples, or make them worse. Be careful not to put too much lotion or cream on your face. That can clog your pores.

## Taking Care of Your Mouth

You know how important it is to brush your teeth. And you already know how your diet affects your teeth. But you should also know that your mouth changes during puberty. The hormones you produce change the acids in your mouth. You are more likely to get bad breath. You also eat different kinds of foods as you get older. These foods can be harder on your teeth. That is why it is important to brush regularly. It is also good to floss. Flossing cleans out small pieces of food from between your teeth and gums. Floss is like thin string. Ask your dentist how to floss properly.

Flossing and brushing regularly will help you keep your mouth in good shape. It will help keep your breath fresh. And you will get fewer cavities.

## Voice Changes

The last major change we will talk about is voice cracking. Sorry, this is one change you can't do anything about.

At some point you will speak to someone and your voice will wobble. It may sound as if you are suddenly speaking in a very high voice. You can't control it. And it's pretty embarrassing. This is called *voice cracking*. Your voice cracks because of your hormones. Your hormones are making your voice box (*larynx*) larger. As your larynx gets larger, your voice gets deeper. Your vocal cords are stretching as your larynx grows. This stretching causes your voice to go up and down.

## Talking with Others about What Puberty Is Like

Voice cracking can be embarrassing. But nearly everyone feels embarrassed during puberty. It's part of becoming an adult. It may help if you remember that every young man's voice changed as he grew up. And it may help to talk to older people about their experiences with puberty. Try asking your dad or your brother about when his voice started cracking. Talk to your uncle, or your coach, about the first time he shaved. Hearing the experiences of others will make you feel better about the changes that are happening to you.

Becoming sexually active also means taking responsibility for birth control and the other person's feelings.

# Chapter 4

## New Responsibilities and Pressures

As you grow older, you must be more responsible. If you are sexually active, you and your partner must act responsibly. That is because sex can have many consequences (outcomes). You can cause a woman to become pregnant. You can transmit a disease through sex. And you can hurt someone's feelings if you do not handle a relationship properly. All these things may make sex sound terrible. Sex can be one of the most enjoyable feelings. It can make you feel wonderful. Being responsible about sex means being careful. It doesn't mean being scared or worried.

*43*

## Birth Control

Preventing pregnancy is not only a woman's job. As a man you are just as responsible for birth control. Many men think that pregnancy is the woman's problem. But this is not true. It takes a man and a woman together to create a child.

There are many ways to have sex without risking pregnancy. Birth control devices (*contraceptives*) are used to prevent pregnancy. There are many different kinds of contraceptives. Some are used by the man. Others are used by the woman.

## Condoms

Condoms are widely available. You can buy them in any drugstore. A *condom* is a thin rubber tube that you slip over your erect penis. The tube catches the semen when it is ejaculated from the penis. The condom stops the semen from entering the woman's vagina. The condom is very reliable. And it is safe and easy to use. A condom should only be put on an erect penis. A condom cannot be used more than once. After ejaculation the penis should come out of the vagina. The condom should then be removed. The penis should be wiped clean. The penis should not go back into the vagina again (unless another condom is put on for more intercourse).

## Other Contraceptives

There are many birth control devices for women. One of the most popular is the *birth control pill.* It must be taken every day. The pill releases hormones in the woman's body that prevent pregnancy. The pill is highly reliable. If a woman takes the pill every day, no other contraceptive is necessary. The pill is a prescription contraceptive. That means you have to see a doctor to get the pill.

Another very popular birth control device is the *diaphragm.* A diaphragm is a rubber cap that is inserted into the vagina. It fits over the entrance to the uterus. The entrance is called the *cervix.* The cap blocks sperm from entering the uterus. The diaphragm must be covered with contraceptive jelly before it is inserted. The jelly gives the protection. It contains a chemical that kills sperm (a *spermicide*). A diaphragm is inserted before sex. It should be left in for a number of hours after sex. The diaphragm is a very reliable method of birth control. A woman needs to see a doctor to get a diaphragm. That is because a diaphragm must be fitted to the size of a woman's cervix.

Drugstores carry many kinds of *contraceptive creams, jellies, and foams.* They are put into the vagina before sex. Most of these products are to be used *with* a condom or a diaphragm.

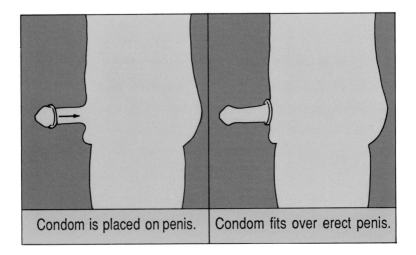

| Condom is placed on penis. | Condom fits over erect penis. |

Alone, these products are not highly reliable methods of birth control. The pill, and the diaphragm or condom (especially if used with a spermicide), are excellent. And they are good for teens. They are not too expensive. They are easy to find. And they are easy to use.

For more information about birth control, ask your librarian for *Everything You Need to Know About Birth Control.*

## Sexually Transmitted Diseases (STDs)

The more you know about the person you have sex with, the safer you will be. That is because you will have less chance of getting an STD. Find out about your partner's background and past sex life. STDs are passed very easily from one person to another. You can tell if a person is a "high risk" by talking to him or her. Then you can decide for yourself if you want to become sexually involved.

STDs are diseases that are passed from one person to another during sex. Some STDs are viruses, like a cold or the flu. Some STDs are caused by bacteria, like other infections.

Remember this warning about the danger of STDs: "When you have sex with a partner, you are having sex with everyone else she or he ever had sex with." That means that your partner could have gotten an STD from someone he or she had sex with. It could have been someone ten years ago. It could have been someone last week. And if they have been exposed to an STD, they could give it to you. There are many STDs. Some are more dangerous than others.

AIDS is an STD. AIDS is a virus. AIDS can kill. At this time there is no cure for AIDS. It is passed from one person to another through blood or semen. When two people have sex, they exchange body fluids. The fluid is usually semen from orgasm. It can also be a very small portion of blood.

You have probably heard that AIDS kills mostly gay men (homosexuals). But gay men are not the only people who can get AIDS. Many people who take drugs and share needles are likely to get AIDS. Children can be born with AIDS from their mothers. Married men and women can get AIDS, too. ANYONE CAN GET AIDS.

There are many other STDs. These are often referred to as "VD." That stands for *venereal disease,* which is another way to say "STD." Most STDs are not as serious as AIDS. Other STDs include *syphilis, gonorrhea,* and *chlamydia.* They are very common. *Genital warts* and *herpes* are two more STDs. These are caused by very common viruses. For more information about STDs, ask your librarian for *Everything You Need to Know About STDs.*

There are ways to reduce your chances of getting an STD. Remember:

• The more often you change partners, the greater your risk.

• Learn about your partner.

• Condoms can protect against STDs.

Condoms form a shield between partners. The shield stops semen from entering your partner's body. And it also stops you from exchanging fluids with your partner. If you don't exchange fluids, you greatly reduce your risks.

All this talk sounds scary. And sex sounds awfully dangerous. But this talk is not meant to frighten you. It is to teach you how to protect yourself and to be responsible. If you know and trust your sex partners, you will be safer. If you use condoms, you will be much safer.

# Chapter 5

## There Are Many Ways to Be a Man

Many people will try to tell you how to be a man. They will tell you how you have to look. You may be told what to do to prove you are a man. Those people are not being fair. How you act is your choice. You should feel comfortable with yourself. And you should be happy with the choices you make.

It is not easy ignoring your friends. Often they will pressure you to look or act a certain way. Sometimes you will feel like doing what they want. And sometimes you won't. When you don't feel like doing what your friends tell you, *don't.* Keep an image of yourself the way you want to be.

Television shows, commercials, and movies can often give you false ideas about how men and women act.

## What Will They Be Telling You?

There are some common messages. Some people will tell you that men are strong and brave. Other people will try to convince you that men are daring and dangerous. You will see ads that tell you a man should always have a woman on each arm. And you will see movies that make you believe that men don't cry or show emotion. But these messages are unfair to you. They make you think there is only one way to be a man. And they make you think that you are less of a man if you do not follow these ideas.

Men can cry. And men can like poetry instead of football. Men can—and should—be kind and gentle. And they can be careful and quiet. These things don't make anyone less of a man. And they can make someone more of a person.

## Homosexuality

*Heterosexuality* means people of different sexes having sex together. *Homosexuality* means people of the same sex having sex together. Homosexuals are also called *gay.* Gay sex is different from heterosexual sex. If two men have sex, there is no vagina. If two women have sex, there is no penis. But there are many other ways to have sex.

Men who are kind and gentle are just as much men as those who act tough and brave.

There are many opinions about homosexuality. Some people say it is not normal behavior. Other people say it is wrong or sinful. But many people today accept homosexuality. And many people believe being gay is just a different way of having sexual feelings.

You have probably heard some people tell you what homosexuals are like. Those people probably talked about a *stereotype*. A stereotype is a general description used to refer to a wide range of people. Many times a stereotype is negative. And it never gives a real picture. Maybe someone told you that gay men are weak, silly, and dress in pink. That is a stereotype. In fact, many gay men are bodybuilders. Many ride motorcycles. And many gay men have done very heroic things. Gay men have as many different characteristics as men who are not gay.

It is normal to wonder at least once in your life if you are a homosexual. You may even think about having a homosexual experience. That is also normal.

If you are like most boys, some of these thoughts may worry you. It is important to talk about your fears to people you trust. Listen to their opinions. And consider their advice. But remember that your sex life is your choice.

## Rambo and Bill Cosby: Two Types of Men

Movies and television show us many different types of men. Sylvester Stallone played Rambo in the movies. Rambo is strong and brave. He fears no danger. He never cries or whines about his life. He runs around the world without a shirt. This is to show everyone his manly muscles. Rambo shows us a common vision of manhood.

Now think about Bill Cosby for a minute. He plays Doctor Huxtable on "The Cosby Show." What sort of a man is he? Dr. Huxtable is a kind and gentle man. He loves being with his wife and children. And he shows his emotions. If he is hurt, he shows people his feelings. He is also a good doctor. He spends his life trying to make people feel better.

There are many other popular men on television and in the movies. Each shows you another kind of manliness. You may like Rambo and Bill Cosby at the same time. That's fine. The important thing is to see that they are each just one type of man. Neither one is more of a man than the other.

# Chapter 6

---

# Some Answers to Some Very Common Questions

Sex and puberty can be a big mystery. When puberty begins, there are many new things to learn about yourself and others. You will get new information about your body and about other people's bodies. It is always good to ask questions. Learning about your body will make you more comfortable with yourself. It will make you more comfortable about sex. And it will make you a happier person.

Here are some questions often asked by young men in puberty.

**My breasts are swollen. And I can feel a small lump under my breasts. Am I turning into a girl?**

No. Swollen breasts are common. So are the lumps. Your body is reacting to the hormones that are being released. The condition may last a while, but don't worry. It will go away.

**Can a penis be too big or too small to fit into a vagina?**

No. Vaginas are not hollow, like the inside of a tunnel. They are more like collapsed balloons. They can expand to fit any size penis.

**I think my penis is too small. What's the normal size?**

A grown man's penis is between 3 1/4 and 4 1/4 inches long. With an erection, the average penis length is 5 to 7 inches. Nine out of ten men have penises around 6 1/4 inches long when erect. Some penises are small when they are relaxed. But they grow when they become erect. Other penises stay fairly long while relaxed. They may not grow very much when erect. Each penis is different.

**Sometimes my penis and testicles hurt. Is there something wrong?**

It is common for your penis and testicles to ache during puberty. It is a reaction to all the growing and changing they are doing. Your testicles may ache if you have an erection for a long time. Sometimes they ache more if you have an erection without ejaculation. This is sometimes called "blue balls." It is caused by a buildup of semen. When you have an erection for a while, your body gets ready to ejaculate.

Sperm build up in the ampulla. If you do not ejaculate, the sperm remains. Sometimes this causes some discomfort.

## Can you have sex without orgasm?

Yes. It is possible that you will not become excited enough to ejaculate. Something may stop you from relaxing enough to ejaculate. Being very nervous can prevent erection or ejaculation. Alcohol and drugs can also change your ability to have sex. Alcohol can make your body less sensitive. It can often make it difficult to get an erection or to ejaculate.

## Can you ejaculate without an erection?

Generally not. The penis must be hard to create pressure. The pressure pushes the semen out of the erect penis during ejaculation.

## I have little white spots on my penis. Do I have an STD?

Those little white spots are most likely from the sweat or oil glands on your penis. They are normal. Sometimes those glands or pores become irritated. They can cause pimples on your penis. Those pimples will probably go away after a few days. If they don't, see a doctor. If you have any reason to believe you may have an STD, see a doctor as soon as possible.

## Is it true that bad things happen to you if you masturbate?

There are many warnings about masturbation. But none of them are true. If you masturbate you will NOT:

- get hair on your palms
- go blind
- have your penis fall off
- become insane
- run out of sperm

The desire to masturbate is normal. And masturbation is safe if you do not use any dangerous objects or substances to masturbate.

## Can you have sex without foreplay?

It is possible, but it is not a good idea. To have good sex, both partners must be ready. Often it takes a woman longer to become ready than a man. Many men think foreplay is just for giving the man an erection. That is not true. Foreplay is also to get the woman ready. When a woman is ready her vagina will be moist and lubricated. That will make sex more enjoyable for both partners.

## Can a girl have sex during her period?

A woman can have sex any time. Her period is just a time when her body is getting rid of an egg that was not fertilized. There is no real reason to avoid sex during this time.

**Can a girl get pregnant with her period?**

YES. If you don't use birth control you can get pregnant any time. Periods happen at different times each month. And sometimes a woman can have some bleeding without it being her period.

**Can a girl get pregnant the first time?**

YES. Any time you have sex, you can get pregnant. And yes, a girl can get pregnant if she has sex standing up.

**How does a woman have an orgasm?**

A woman has an orgasm when her *clitoris* is excited. The clitoris is located under the lips of the vagina. The clitoris is similar to a penis. When the clitoris is excited it releases some fluids. And it causes muscles to spasm. Many men think a long or a thick penis produces an orgasm more easily. This is not true. Orgasm has nothing to do with penis size. Orgasm is caused by exciting the clitoris. This occurs when the penis rubs against it during sex.

**Can a girl get pregnant if you don't put your penis inside?**

This is a hard question to answer. There is always a chance of pregnancy whenever the genitals of a man and a woman touch. When you have an erection, some semen may drip out of the penis before ejaculation. It is possible to get some semen on or in the woman. The chances of pregnancy are very slim this way, but it is not impossible.

## Can you get AIDS from kissing someone?

AIDS kills many thousands of people each year. But there are only a few ways you can get AIDS.

You *can* get AIDS if you:

- share a needle with someone who has AIDS
- have sex with a person who has AIDS (though you'll be much safer if you use a condom)
- have an open infection that comes into contact with the blood of someone with AIDS
- are born with AIDS (because your mother passed it to you through the bloodstream).

You *cannot* get AIDS from:

- toilet seats or doorknobs
- kissing
- touching someone with AIDS.

# Glossary—*Explaining New Words*

**acne** Severe skin problem that causes infected pimples.

**AIDS** An STD virus that can cause death.

**blackhead** A pimple caused by sebum exposed to air.

**circumcision** Trimming of the foreskin.

**clitoris** Female sex organ that gets excited to orgasm during sex.

**condom** A rubber shield that is placed over an erect penis.

**contraceptives** Birth control devices.

**ejaculation** Pushing semen from the penis.

**erection** When the penis becomes hard and stiff.

**fallopian tubes** Tubes that carry the egg from the ovaries to the uterus.

**fertilized** When the egg and sperm unite and start to grow.

**foreplay** Time of kissing and touching before intercourse.

**foreskin** Skin over the head of the penis.

**gay** Homosexual.

**genes** Chemicals that tell your body how to grow.

**glands** Organs that produce different liquids and chemicals, such as hormones.

**heterosexual** A person who has sex with persons of the opposite sex.

**homosexual** A person who has sex with others of the same sex.

**hormones** Chemicals that cause changes in the body.

**masturbation** Exciting yourself, usually the genitals.

**puberty** A time of change for the body

**reproduce** Have children.

**sanitary napkins** Pads used to absorb blood during menstruation.

**scrotum** The sac under the penis.

**semen** Fluid pushed from the penis during ejaculation; contains sperm.

**smegma** Substance released from glands that can build up under the foreskin. Can cause irritation.

**sperm** Male fertilizers.

**spermicides** Creams, foams, or jellies that kill sperm.

**STDs** Diseases passed through sex.

**stereotype** A general statement applied to a group of people. Often negative.

**tampon** A roll of absorbent paper and fiber used internally during menstruation.

**testicles** Organs that produce sperm.

**testosterone** Male hormone.

**urinary opening** Slit that passes urine and semen.

**uterus** The womb. Houses a fertilized egg.

**vagina** Opening that leads to the uterus.

**vas deferens** Tube that carries sperm.

**VD** Venereal disease, or STD.

# For Further Reading

Gale, Jay, Ph.D. *A Young Man's Guide to Sex.* Los Angeles: Price, Stern, Sloan, 1988.

Hughes, Tracy. *Everything You Need to Know About Teen Pregnancy.* New York: The Rosen Publishing Group, 1988.

Madaras, Lynda. *The What's Happening to My Body? Book for Boys.* New York: Newmarket Press, 1988.

Mucciolo, Gary, M.D. *Everything You Need to Know About Birth Control.* New York: The Rosen Publishing Group, 1988.

Taylor, Barbara. *Everything You Need to Know About AIDS.* New York: The Rosen Publishing Group, 1988.

Wesson, Carolyn McLenahan. *Teen Troubles: How to Keep Them From Becoming Tragedies.* New York: Walker and Company, 1988.

Woods, Samuel G. *Everything You Need to Know About STD.* New York: The Rosen Publishing Group, 1990.

# Index

**About the Author**
Bruce Glassman has authored over twelve books for young adults and
has been a staff writer on two Connecticut newspapers. He currently
lives in New Haven, Connecticut, where he is a book editor and a
freelance writer.

**About the Editor**
Evan Stark is a well-known sociologist, educator, and therapist—as well
as a popular lecturer on women's and children's health issues. Dr. Stark
was the Henry Rutgers Fellow at Rutgers University, and associate at the
Institution for Social and Policy Studies at Yale University, and a
Fulbright Fellow at the University of Essex. He is the author of many
publications in the field of family relations and is the father of four
children.

**Acknowledgments and Photo Credits**
Cover photo by Chuck Peterson
Photographs on pages 2, 8, 18, 33, 39, 42, 51, Barbara Kirk; page 36 Stuart Rabinowitz;
Arton pages 13, 22, 27, 46, Sonja Kalter

Design/Production: Blackbirch Graphics, Inc.